ROCK YOUR REAL ESTATE BUSINESS

The Power of Referrals and Rewards

Mini Mastery Series

Donna Wysinger

Copyright 2025 © Be a Better Agent

Copyright Notice

Rock Your Real Estate Business:
The Power of Referrals and Rewards
Copyright © 2025 by Be a Better Agent
All rights reserved.

No part of this book may be reproduced, stored in a retrieval system, or transmitted in any form or by any means; electronic, mechanical, photocopying, recording, or otherwise, without prior written permission from the author, except for brief quotations used in a review.

This book is intended for informational and personal use only. The author and publisher are not responsible for any actions or outcomes resulting from the use of the content within. The exercises and prompts are meant to inspire creativity and positive business practices and should not replace professional advice when needed.

ISBN: 979-8-9930660-0-4

Be a Better Agent

For permissions, inquiries, or further information, visit beabetteragent.com

To all of the real estate brokers, team leaders, and mentors in my life ...

Thank you for your guidance, generosity, and belief in me. The lessons you have shared have shaped the way I show up in this business and inspired me to pass that wisdom forward.

This book is for you and those you continue to inspire.

To my incredible clients, family, and friends ...

Your trust, encouragement, business, and referrals have been the foundation of my business and the heart of my success. I am forever grateful for the opportunity to serve, grow, and thrive alongside you.

This book is because of you.

Thank you.

TABLE OF CONTENTS

INTRODUCTION: *Why Referrals ROCK!*   1
The power of a relationship-based business and how this guide will help you grow one with ease and joy.

CHAPTER 1: *Set Your Intention to ROCK It!*   5
Ground your mindset, energy, and actions in a clear vision of referral-based success.

CHAPTER 2: *Who Is in Your REFERRAL Circle?*   15
Identify your existing advocates and potential partners already cheering you on.

CHAPTER 3: *Ask Like a PRO … Without Feeling Weird*   23
Scripts, strategies, and mindset shifts that make asking for referrals feel natural and aligned.

CHAPTER 4: *The MAGIC of Meaningful REWARDS*   31
Creative and thoughtful ways to say thank you … the kind people never forget.

CHAPTER 5: *Fabulous Follow-Up Systems*   41
Build in consistency, gratitude, and delight with simple, sustainable systems.

CHAPTER 6: *Shine the SPOTLIGHT on Your Referrers*   49
Celebrate and elevate the people who support your business publicly and personally.

TABLE OF CONTENTS

CHAPTER 7: *Partnering for POWER* — 57
Strategic alliances and community collaborations that multiply your reach.

CHAPTER 8: *Events that SPARK Referrals* — 65
Easy-to-execute, joyful events that create buzz, memories, and connections.

CHAPTER 9: *Market with a REFERRAL MINDSET* — 73
Show up consistently with visibility strategies rooted in trust and value.

CHAPTER 10: *Keep Up the MOMENTUM* — 81
Set goals, review and refresh your program, stay engaged, and keep it easeful

CONCLUSION: *Building a Business with HEART* — 89
Why referrals aren't just a strategy, they're a movement. You're building something bigger than yourself.

MORE MAGIC: *Bonus Materials* — 93

- Reward Ideas for Every Budget
- 12 Months of Referral Marketing Ideas
- Sample Pop-By Ideas
- Real Estate Referral Roadmap
- Self-Care for the Referral Rockstar

Foreword

If you've ever built a business that felt more like a calling, you already know. It's not just about sales. It's about connection. It's about showing up in people's lives in ways that matter. Over my years in real estate, I've discovered that the most joyful, sustainable, and soul-aligned way to grow is through referrals rooted in trust, kindness, and genuine appreciation. That's what this book is all about: creating a business you love, powered by the people who love working with you.

This guide was born from the belief that we don't have to hustle our way to success. We can flow there. With creativity, intention, and a LOT of gratitude, we can turn every client experience into something worth sharing—and every referral into a reason to celebrate. Whether you're just starting out or looking to infuse new energy into your business, I hope these pages feel like a conversation between friends.

My wish is that you not only walk away with ideas, tools, and understanding, but with the confidence to lead your business with heart. Because when you do? The magic happens.

Let's do this ... together.

Donna Wysinger
Owner/Founder
Be a Better Agent

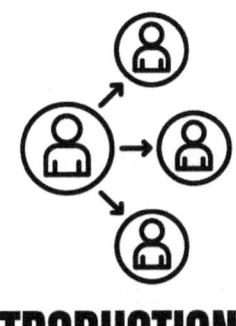

INTRODUCTION

Why Referrals ROCK

There's Something Magic about Receiving Referrals

It's not just a name or a lead. It's a gift wrapped in trust, loyalty, and belief in your ability to serve.

In today's fast-paced world, where advertising and marketing are so important, and also time consuming and expensive, where cold calling and online leads can feel cold and disconnected, a referral is a warm handoff.

A referral tells you, *"This is someone I care about, and I trust you to take good care of them."*

 Real Estate with Heart (and Soul)

Let's be real. We didn't get into real estate to shuffle paperwork or put out yard signs. One of the main reasons we do what we do is that we love helping people make life-changing moves.

We love the energy of new beginnings, the satisfaction of solving problems, and the joy of saying, "*Welcome Home.*"

A referral-based business allows you to grow in a way that's not only effective but connects you with your friends, clients, and community. It builds something bigger than just a brand — it builds a movement of people who believe in you and want to see you succeed.

When the Phone Rings Because of YOU

"Hi! my friend told me to call you — they said you're the best!" Is there anything better?

When someone thinks of you first when real estate comes up, you've reached a powerful point in your business. That moment isn't luck. It's earned. It's the result of your care, your service, and your connections.

Here's the Key . . .

You can multiply that magic intentionally, by creating a system that turns casual support into consistent referrals. You can teach your friends, family, and clients HOW to refer in the best way possible. You can turn those who refer to you into heroes AND increase your return on those referrals in a way that makes everyone happy!

Trust is earned, referrals are PROOF.

☹ The Lesson I Didn't Want

When I first became an agent, *(around 25 years ago, but who's counting?)*, I found out very quickly that almost everything I learned in *"real estate"* school was not the information I would need to grow my real estate business. After earning my license and finding a brokerage, the first thing I tried to learn was how to generate leads. Every class I took (and some came highly recommended) taught me the most important lesson of all: cold calling, and knocking on doors, and running ads … just made me cry.

The Lesson I Needed

I needed to build a *"Referral-Based Business"* to succeed, but traditional requests for referrals didn't work *(like those lines on so many business cards, "The biggest compliment I can receive…blah, blah.")* … You get the idea.

I started teaching my SOI *(sphere of influence)* how to refer to me, then I rewarded them again and again, from first contact, through the transaction process, to closing the deal. Then it happened again, and those happy clients learned how to refer and brought me even more referrals!

👩 From Tears to Cheers!

I still remember the first time I received a call from a former client I hadn't seen in months who said, *"My friend from work needs to buy a house and you are the only one I trust."* **Yay! Success!!**

📘 What This Guide Will Teach You

It took some time and a lot of trial and error for me to learn what this how-to Mini Mastery guide will teach you in just an hour or two.

This guide is your **step-by-step blueprint** to build a thriving, enjoyable, referral-powered real estate business. You will learn how to:

- Ask for referrals in a way that feels natural *(not awkward)*
- Build a rewards system that people love and keeps them referring
- Maintain top-of-mind status in ways that are meaningful, not salesy
- Make your clients feel like VIPs. Because they are!

Whether you're a brand new agent or a seasoned pro, this guide will help you deepen relationships, expand your reach, and grow your business with ease, success, and a lot of fun.

Let's Do This 👊👊

Get ready to ROCK your real estate business. Not through hustle or pressure, but through connection, gratitude, and the joy of helping others.

Let's turn one referral into many. Let's grow your business by celebrating the people who believe in you. Let's get started!

CHAPTER 1
Set Your Intention to ROCK It!

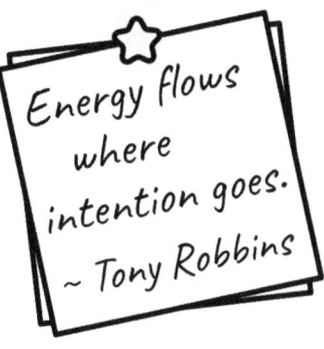

Energy flows where intention goes.
~ Tony Robbins

Before we dive into rewards, referral programs, and fun events, we will start with the foundation of success: **your intention**.

Why? Because a referral-based business isn't just a marketing strategy, it is a:

 **Mindset**  **Mission**  **Movement**

When you decide that referrals will be the heartbeat of your business, you begin to show up differently. You focus on connection instead of conversion. Your intention is service rather than selling. And in return? People feel it. And they remember you.

Why Intention Matters

In real estate, it's easy to get swept up in the day-to-day grind: lead generation, showings, deadlines, paperwork, follow-up, follow-up, follow-up...

But when you pause to set a powerful intention, **"I attract loyal, happy clients who refer me with joy,"** you start to attract business in a way that feels easier, more aligned. And yes, even more fun.

Think of your intention as the **North Star** of your business. You don't need to hustle in every direction. You just need to stay aligned with your WHY.

✦ Choose Your North Star

Here are a few powerful intentions to inspire your own:

- "I build my business through generosity and trust."
- "Referrals flow to me with ease because I care deeply for my clients."
- "I turn clients into friends, and friends into advocates."
- "I deliver an experience so good, they can't wait to tell others."
- "I celebrate every referral like the gift it is."

Take a moment to write your own intention:

My Referral-Based Business Intention

_____
_____
_____
_____
_____
_____

Get Clear on Your Referral Vision

Now, let's get a little more practical.

Setting intention isn't just about mindset. It's also about clarity. And clarity creates confidence.

Answer these questions for yourself:

- How many referrals would I LOVE to receive per month?
- Who are my top 10-25 people most likely to send me referrals?
- How do I plan to stay in touch with them?
- How will I reward and celebrate their referrals?

My Top Referral Power Partners

Write the names, contact information, and notes for 6 - 8 of your Power Partners. These are the people that, if asked, would sing your praises and bring their friends and family to YOU.

NAME: _____

PHONE: _____

EMAIL: _____

NOTES: _____

_____

_____

_____

NAME: _____

PHONE: _____

EMAIL: _____

NOTES: _____

_____

_____

_____

NAME: _____
PHONE: _____
EMAIL: _____
NOTES: _____
_____
_____

NAME: _____
PHONE: _____
EMAIL: _____
NOTES: _____
_____
_____

NAME: _____
PHONE: _____
EMAIL: _____
NOTES: _____
_____
_____

NAME: _____
PHONE: _____
EMAIL: _____
NOTES: _____

_____

_____

NAME: _____
PHONE: _____
EMAIL: _____
NOTES: _____

_____

_____

NAME: _____
PHONE: _____
EMAIL: _____
NOTES: _____

_____

_____

Set Your Referral Goals

Let's break it down into simple numbers. A strong referral-based business often follows this rhythm:

- 1 in 10 people in your sphere will give you a referral each year (minimum).
- The more intentional your connection + reward system, the higher that ratio becomes.

So if you truly nurture 100 people in your network:

▶▶ **You can expect 10+ solid referrals a year.**

Want 24 transactions a year from referrals?

▶▶ **Nurture 200–250 people with heart and purpose.**

And don't worry. This doesn't mean cold calls or weekly check-ins. It means genuine, generous touches spread throughout the year. This guide will give you lots of ideas!

Align Your Energy, Actions & Expectations

This isn't about pushing harder. It's about becoming magnetic. When your **energy aligns with your purpose,** and your **actions reflect your care,** you naturally create a business that flows.

- People **want** to refer you.
- They **feel good** doing it.
- They're **excited** to connect others to someone they trust.

🔑 Key Reflections

How do I want to show up in the world as a real estate professional?

_____
_____
_____
_____

What would it feel like if referrals flowed to me with joy, ease, and abundance?

_____
_____
_____
_____

What's one step I can take this week to align with that vision?

_____
_____
_____
_____

You've Got This!

NOTES

DOODLES

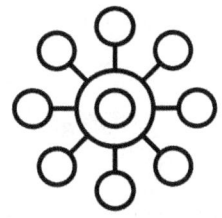

CHAPTER 2

Who Is In Your
REFERRAL Circle?

Referrals don't just come from past clients. They come from **relationships**. And those relationships are all around you, some obvious, some waiting to be discovered.

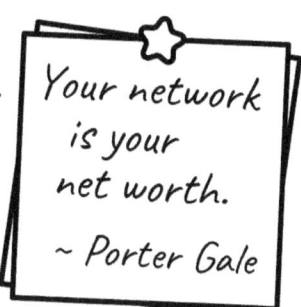

Your network is your net worth.
~ Porter Gale

The goal of this chapter is to help you **map your referral ecosystem** ... the people who know you, like you, trust you, and would be thrilled to recommend you if they were just a little more **aware** ... and a little more *reminded*.

💰 Your Sphere of Influence = Your Goldmine

Your sphere of influence is everyone you're connected to, either personally or professionally. It includes:

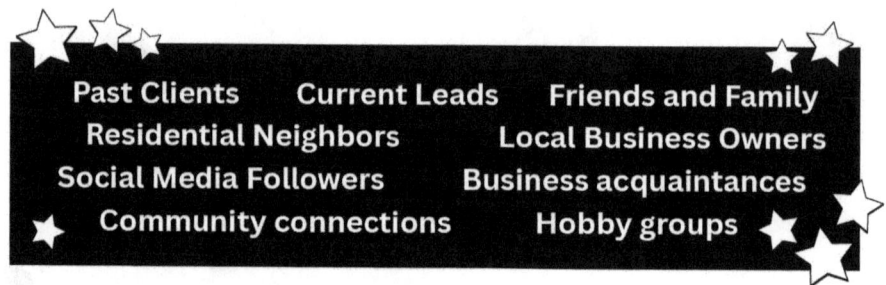

Past Clients   Current Leads   Friends and Family
Residential Neighbors   Local Business Owners
Social Media Followers   Business acquaintances
Community connections   Hobby groups

If someone knows who you are, they are in your sphere. And if you've ever made them feel seen, heard, or supported ... they could become a referral source.

 Your Champions, Connectors, and Cheerleaders

Within your sphere are three golden categories of people:

Champions
These are your **raving fans**. They've worked with you, loved the experience, and already refer people your way. Treat them like royalty, because they are!

Connectors
These people know **_everyone_**. They might not refer as often, but when they do, it's golden. Think: local business owners, hair stylists, yoga instructors, networking pros, and community leaders.

Cheerleaders
These are your **enthusiastic supporters**. They may not know a lot of buyers or sellers but they believe in you and love to spread the word. They'll share your social media posts, hype you up at parties, and celebrate your success from the sidelines.

Each of these groups deserves to be nurtured, in many fun and different ways. The rest of this guide will give you dozens of ideas for how to do just that.

Think Beyond Clients

Referrals often come from the least expected people, the ones you see regularly, but may not have on your official *"marketing list."*

Here are just a few non-client champions to consider:

- **Your hairstylist, barber, or nail tech**
- **Your gym coach, trainer, or yoga instructor**
- **Your favorite barista**
- **Your vet or pet groomer**
- **Your handyman or contractor**
- **Your favorite local shop owner or baker**
- **Your massage therapist, acupuncturist, or doctor**
- **Friends in your book club, band, or hiking group**
- **Neighbors (even if they're not moving!)**
- **Former co-workers or school classmates**
- **Your child's teacher or school admin**

They may not need to move, but they know people who do. And if you're **"Top of Mind"** among these connections, they will refer their friends and family to YOU.

17

Create Your "Top 25" VIP Referral List

Your Top 25 is a hand-picked list of people who are likely to refer you, or already have. These are your VIPs. You'll give them extra love, extra attention, and intentional connection.

What Makes Someone a VIP Top 25?

- They've already referred someone to you
- They're naturally outgoing or network well
- You see or talk to them regularly
- You've built real trust with them
- You love the idea of treating them like a VIP

Name VIP Top 25:

_____ _____
_____ _____
_____ _____
_____ _____
_____ _____
_____ _____
_____ _____
_____ _____
_____ _____
_____ _____
_____ _____
_____ _____

Real Talk: This Isn't Just About Business

Your referral circle isn't just a list. It's a **community of trust.** It's the group of people who believe in you. And that means something.

The more you nurture them, appreciate them, and show up with authenticity, the more they'll want to lift you up and send opportunity your way.

Once you have created your **VIP Top 25** list, ensure you have each one's contact information in your database. You can even group them into their own category so it will be an easy list to access when you market to and connect with them.

Get intentional.

Get excited.

And get ready to connect in ways that flow.

🔑 Key Reflections

Who are some people in my life who already speak highly of me?

_____
_____
_____
_____
_____

Who do I love working with — and want more of?

_____
_____
_____
_____
_____
_____

Who are three people I can reach out to this week to simply reconnect with and thank?

_____
_____
_____

It pays to have friends!

NOTES

DOODLES

CHAPTER 3

Ask Like a PRO
... Without Feeling Weird

You don't get what you don't ask for.
~ Nora Roberts

Let's be honest. Asking for referrals can feel... awkward. No one wants to seem pushy, desperate, or salesy, especially when your brand is built on trust and care.

But here's the truth: **If you've shown up with integrity, delivered value, and created connection, asking isn't weird. It's generous.** You're giving people a chance to support you. And that helps THEM feel good.

You are also providing assistance they might be hesitant to ask for. Offering to help their friends and family can open a dialog and also allow them to be the hero when you deliver exemplary service to those they care about.

23

Let's reframe *"the ask"* into something that's honest, kind, and effective.

Crafting Your Referral Request with Heart and Clarity

A great referral request does two things:

✓ **Connects emotionally**

✓ **Makes it easy to say YES**

Here's a simple formula:

> **Warm Greeting + Appreciation + Why You're Asking + How They Can Help + GRATITUDE**

Example:

"Hi Julia! I've been thinking about how much I loved working with you on your home purchase. You were such a joy, and I'm truly grateful you trusted me with such a big moment in your life. If you happen to know anyone else who's thinking of buying or selling, I'd love the chance to help them too. Referrals are how I grow my business, and they mean the world to me. Thank you so much if anyone comes to mind!"

It's that easy.

You're not begging.

You're inviting... with heart.

⏱ Timing and Frequency of the Ask

You don't have to ask every time you talk to someone. But there are natural and perfect times when the ask flows beautifully.

Best Times to Ask:

- After a great closing experience
- When a client thanks you or compliments your service
- On a client's home-buying or home-selling anniversary
- In a follow-up or check-in message
- During a casual catch-up conversation
- When you're sharing market insights or local updates

How Often Should I Ask?

- Think *"light touch, consistent rhythm."*
- Once per quarter in an email
- Monthly mentions in newsletters or social media
- One-on-one as opportunities arise
- Mix it into your normal conversations and marketing — just like planting seeds.

Using Storytelling to Make Your Ask Memorable

Stories spark emotion. Emotion leads to action.

When you show how you helped someone *(instead of just telling)*, people feel why referring you matters.

Instead of this:

> *"Please refer me to anyone you know."*

Try this:

> *"Last month, I helped a single mom with two kids sell her home above asking price and move closer to her family. She had no idea where to start, and by the end, she cried happy tears at the closing table. That's why I love what I do. If you know anyone who could use that kind of support, I'd love to help."*

Big difference, right? Real stories. Real people. Real heart.

Sample Scripts for Every Kind of Ask

Let's make this crazy easy. Here are ready-to-go referral asks for multiple formats:

Text Message Ask:

> *Hey [Name]! I wanted to say thank you again for trusting me with the sale of your home. If you know anyone who is buying or selling in the next few weeks or months, I'd be honored if you would connect them with me. Referrals are how I grow and improve. And they mean so much. And so.do.YOU!*

Email Ask:

Subject Line: A Quick Favor from Your Favorite Realtor

Hi [Name],

I hope you're doing amazingly well! I've been reflecting on the great people I've had the chance to work with, and you're definitely at the top of that list.

My business thrives on referrals, and I'd be so grateful if you think of me first when someone you know is ready to buy or sell a home. I promise to give them the same high-quality experience I gave to you!

Thanks so much... and let's stay in touch!

Warmly,

[Your Name]

Social Media Post:

FUN FACT ... Most of my clients come from referrals, amazing people like YOU who connect me to others who need a trustworthy, helpful real estate partner. Thank you so much to all you who have trusted me with your friends and family. If you are already part of my Referral VIP program, we have some fun events and surprises coming. If you would like to join us, I would be honored to help your loved ones make their next move!

In-Person Ask:

"Who do you know that is ready to sell or buy a home soon? I'd love for you to connect them with me. I'll even show you how easy that is to do. I always make sure the people YOU care about feel supported and taken care of by ME! ... Excellent! I appreciate you so much!"

🔑 Key Reflections

Who are 3-4 people I could confidently ask for a referral right now?

_____ _____

_____ _____

What recent success story could I share to make my ask more meaningful?

_____

_____

_____

_____

_____

_____

Where in my weekly rhythm can I naturally mention referrals?

_____

_____

You've got this. You're not *"asking for a favor."* You're giving people a way to support someone they care about, and support you.

Asking isn't weird. It's wise, warm, and aligned with your purpose.

Let's make it a habit.

NOTES

DOODLES

CHAPTER 4

The MAGIC of Meaningful
REWARDS

"A referral isn't just good for business. It's a gesture of trust, loyalty, and caring. And that's what my business is built on." ~ **Donna**

A little thanks goes a long way.

 Golden Eggs vs. Golden GOOSE

You have probably heard the fable about the goose that lays golden eggs.

A lot of real estate agents get caught up chasing eggs ... the leads, the sales, the next transaction.

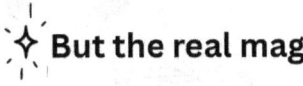 But the real magic?

It's in the goose.

The one that lays the eggs.

In real estate, the *"golden goose"* is your referrer. They are the person who believes in you enough to share your name ... again and again.

The referrer is the one who brings the opportunity, often repeatedly, with care, consistency, and loyalty.

Yes, every referral matters. Every golden egg is a blessing. AND, it's the relationship behind that referral — the golden goose — that deserves the most gratitude, the most attention, and the most love.

So, while you celebrate the referrals that come your way... Remember also to cherish the ones who send them. **They are the foundation of your business.**

The Magic of Referral Rewards

Referrals say:

> *"I trust you to treat MY people like YOUR people."*

That trust deserves more than just the transaction that is conducted with their people. The person who gave you the referral also deserves recognition, appreciation, and a little magic.

You are creating a business rooted in **connection.**

Anyone can send a $10 gift card as a thank you for a referral. However, **your rewards should reflect your brand, your energy, and your gratitude.**

Consider:

★ **Personalized over generic**
★ **Surprising over expected**
★ **Thoughtful over expensive**

When you give from the heart, with even a small gesture, it builds a bond that can last far beyond the gift itself.

🏷️ Tangible Reward Ideas: Thoughtful, Branded, and Fun

Here are some ideas to get your creative rewards juices flowing. Mix and match to fit your brand, your budget, and the personality of the person you are rewarding.

Gift Cards (Local and Loved)

- Their favorite neighborhood coffee shop
- Local restaurant or bakery you've enjoyed together
- Spa, massage, or wellness gift cards
- Pet supply or grooming shops
- Home décor stores *(especially after a closing)*

Physical Gifts with Personality

- Branded candles, mugs, or notepads
- Custom cookies or gourmet treats
- Artisan gifts (Etsy or local markets are great sources)
- Bottle of wine or bubbly with a branded tag
- Home-related goodies (succulents, tea towels, framed quotes, linen sprays, branded utensils)

Exclusive Invitations

- Invitations to VIP events hosted by you or your brokerage
- Annual Client Appreciation Party *(anyone who has referred business to you now has access to any events that you host for your present and former clients)*
- Holiday dessert open house or porch pop-by

People love to feel part of a club or exclusive community, *"You are now part of our Premier Partners Program!"*

Unexpected Delights: The Real Magic

Some of the most meaningful rewards aren't big or flashy. They're unexpected. These little *"just because"* moments often leave the biggest impression.

Handwritten Notes

- A simple, heartfelt thank-you goes a long way.
- Mention what you appreciate about them
- Bonus points if you include a personal detail (*"Hope Lucy's recital went great!"*)

Surprise Porch Drops

- Small seasonal gifts dropped off at their door *(pumpkin bread in fall, sparkling lemonade in summer, cozy cocoa kit in winter)*
- Include a fun tag: *"Just popping by to say thank you for keeping me in mind!"*

Local Favorites

- Drop off or send from a beloved local bakery or shop
- Support a business and surprise your client. Win-win!

Creating a Referral Rewards Program

Ready to take it to the next level? Design a **Referral Rewards Program** that creates buzz, builds loyalty, and encourages more referrals.

Due to local real estate rules and guidelines, you may not be able to ask for referrals. However, you CAN build a reputation for rewarding your referrers.

When you receive a referral, reward the referrer. Whether it turns into a transaction is not the point. **Rewarding the behavior encourages more of the same.**

Remember… the referrer is the *"golden goose."*

Make it fun … Make it you.

Name your program something that has your personality or your vibe:

- **The Referral Circle**
- **Guy's Golden Givers**
- **Kathie's Key Sharers**
- **Spencer's Super Troupe**
- **Trusted Tribe**
- **Gratitude Group**

Always ALWAYS express how grateful you are and how much their support means to you.

🔑 Key Reflections

What kinds of rewards can I give that feel most like ME?

_____
_____
_____
_____
_____
_____
_____
_____

Which clients or friends deserve a surprise thank you right now?

_____
_____
_____
_____
_____
_____
_____

🗝️ Key Reflections

What could my unique referral reward system look like?

_____
_____
_____
_____
_____
_____
_____
_____
_____
_____

Remember: It's not about buying referrals. It's about celebrating relationships and letting people know they matter to you.

When your rewards come from the heart, they'll never feel transactional. **They'll feel transformational.**

So go ahead... plan your surprises, stock your gift cards, design your thank-you notes.

Let the gratitude flow.

NOTES

NOTES

DOODLES

CHAPTER 5

FABULOUS
Follow Up Systems

> *Success ... is built in the follow through.*

If referrals are the life breath of your relationship-based business, then thoughtful follow-up is the steady heartbeat that keeps it alive and thriving. Not the robotic, one-size-fits-all kind we've all experienced, but the kind that feels real, warm, and personal.

We're talking about thoughtful, human-centered, smile-making touchpoints that keep you top of mind, and make people love referring you ... again and again.

Let's explore how to make your follow-up fun, fantastic, and full of heart.

Referral Tracker Tools and Templates

Before we talk about celebration and appreciation, let's make sure you have a system that keeps you organized. You don't need fancy software. You just need a way to track who referred whom, when, and what you've done to thank them. Here are a few easy options:

Paper Tracker or Spreadsheet:

Great for visual thinkers! Create columns for:

- Referrer Name
- Referred Client
- Date Referred
- Outcome (Pending, Closed, Didn't Convert)
- Thank You Sent? (Yes/No)
- Gift/Note Follow-Up

CRM Tags or Pipelines:

Many real estate **CRM** *(Customer Relationship Management)* systems allow you to tag contacts as "Referrer" or add a custom pipeline stage. *(Consider: Follow Up Boss, Wise Agent, Real Geeks, or LionDesk.)*

Online Boards:

Use a drag-and-drop board to track status, notes, and celebration moments. *(Examples: Trello or Notion.)*

Research then choose the option that works best for YOU.

Thank-You Timeline: When and How Often We Show Appreciation

Referrals are not a one-and-done appreciation moment. They deserve ongoing gratitude, because the relationship with your referrer is what you're honoring.

Reward Each Step in the Process

- Give an immediate thank you for the initial referral *(email, text, or call – "Your referral means the world to me!")*

- Mail a handwritten thank-you note with a gift card within 3 days after the referral.

- Send or deliver a small surprise *(gift card, local goodie, or fun real estate-themed treat)* to your referrer when the client agrees to work with you and signs that contract paperwork.

- Give another, bigger heartfelt reward when the new client goes under contract *(VIP gift, a dinner invite, or an upgrade in your rewards program)*.

- Celebrate BIG with your referrer when the client closes. *(Entered into a drawing for a weekend getaway or high-value gift, added to your "Top Referrers" list with special perks.)*

Continued Gratitude and Recognition

- Show your gratitude in your newsletter or social media.
- Continue adding little surprises and shout outs to show you're still grateful.

 Celebrating Birthdays, Home Anniversaries and "Just Because" Moments

Keeping relationships warm is the secret to becoming unforgettable. Don't wait for holidays to reappear in someone's life. Here are moments that are made for follow-up love:

Birthdays:

Send a fun card, a short video message, or a gift card to a VIP's favorite local spot.

Home Anniversaries:

When you send recognition for a home sale or buy to a client, why not send a little something to celebrate the day with the referrer as well? A postcard, flower drop, or coffee treat can be a gentle reminder that you are always ready to receive more referrals … and it will also brighten your referrer's day because you are thinking of them.

"Thinking of You" Days:

No occasion needed! Random acts of appreciation like a handwritten card or small goodie to build surprise delight.

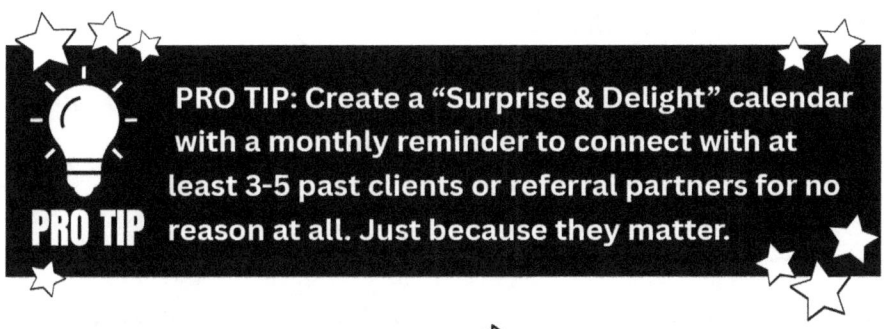

PRO TIP: Create a "Surprise & Delight" calendar with a monthly reminder to connect with at least 3-5 past clients or referral partners for no reason at all. Just because they matter.

Automating with Authenticity

As your business grows, you will have more and more to do and will require some automation in order to organize your efforts. Systems are key to making sure everything is remembered and handled. This isn't about being robotic, it's about freeing up your time so you can make space for genuine, thoughtful connections. Here's how you can do it with heart:

- Use calendar reminders to follow up on birthdays, closings, and referrals.
- Set up automated emails with personal-feeling messaging *(like: "Just checking in to say hi!")*.
- Use a service *(Postable, Handwrytten, SendOutCards)* to send real cards with your handwriting, or pictures of your VIP *(gleaned from past events or social media)*. They will enjoy receiving a heartfelt message from you in a card with a picture of their house, or their pet!

Use Canva templates to create branded note cards, postcards, or client appreciation materials in advance. Then just add those pics and heartfelt messages when needed.

🔑 Key Reflections

How do you currently track and celebrate your referrals?

_____
_____
_____
_____
_____

What could you add or automate to make your follow-up more consistent and meaningful?

_____
_____
_____
_____
_____
_____

What's one "just because" surprise you could send or deliver this month?

_____
_____

Now it's time to make your follow-up fun, fabulous, and full of heart. **You've got this!**

NOTES

DOODLES

CHAPTER 6

Shine the SPOTLIGHT
On Your Referrers

Imagine this: You refer someone to a business you believe in, and that business turns around and celebrates you. Not just with a thank-you note, but with real recognition. That's powerful. It affirms your effort, your trust, and your value in the relationship.

> *People love to feel appreciated and seen.*

Referrers are more than just names in your CRM database. They are your advocates, your ambassadors, your inner circle. When you shine a spotlight on them in ways that feel meaningful, others want to step into that light too.

This chapter is all about how to celebrate your champions out loud ... with creativity, authenticity, and heart.

📱 Social Media Shoutouts (With Permission)

A quick, thoughtful public thank you can go a long way, especially on social media. It not only shows your appreciation but also boosts the confidence of your referrer and inspires others to join in.

Here's how to do it well:

- Tag your referrer *(with permission)* and thank them by name.
- Mention how grateful you are and how much it means to receive referrals.
- Keep it personal, not salesy.
- Use a friendly photo, simple graphic, or even a short video.

Example Post:

> "Thank you for referring The Harper family to me. I am looking SO forward to working with them! And I hope you enjoy your gift card to Pat's Barbecue. I know you LOVE their ribs! Just my way of saying, Thank you SO much for your referral!"

VIP of the Month Program ⭐

Feature a standout referrer each month *(or quarter)* and give them the spotlight they deserve! This is a great way to build loyalty and deepen connections.

Title ideas:

- Referral Rockstar
- You Made My Month
- Gratitude Spotlight
- Spring Referral All-Star

Ways to Make it Shine:

- Share their photo *(with consent)*, a fun fact about them, or a quote.
- Add a reward: a local gift card, a sweet treat, or exclusive invite.
- Frame it in a way that celebrates who they are, not just what they did.
- Hire a local yard sign business to post, *"Thank you! I am grateful for YOU!"* These signs are colorful and fun and can even be personalized and show your appreciation in a BIG way!

Each referral you receive gives you a lovely opportunity to celebrate and share your gratitude out loud.

Stories That Make Others Want to Be Featured

One of the best ways to grow referrals? Tell stories of the amazing people who already refer you.

Share a sweet narrative that paints a picture:

> *"Lisa referred her neighbor who had just lost her partner and needed someone gentle and clear to help her move forward. I was honored to be that person. Lisa's trust gave me the opportunity to serve someone during a difficult time. I was honored to be a part of the process."*

Stories like this:

- Encourage empathy and connection.
- Reinforce the emotional why behind your work.
- Subtly invite others to think of who in their life could use your help.

When people see others being appreciated for referring ... they want to join the celebration.

Create a Referral Wall of Fame

A fun, visual way to honor the people who support your business, you can do this physically or digitally.

Ideas for a "Wall of Fame":

- A corkboard in your office with photos or names of referrers
- A framed poster that grows as names are added
- A dedicated highlight or a pinned social media post
- A digital honor roll in your email newsletter

You could include:

- Number of referrals *(like little stars)*
- Favorite treat or activity
- Why they're amazing
- A quote from you about what their referral meant

This builds community, not just a contact list. You are demonstrating that your business is powered by more than just transactions. **The relationships are the key.**

The Real Reward - Feeling Seen

The greatest reward you can offer isn't always monetary, it's acknowledgment. Your people want to feel that their efforts to support you **mattered**.

When someone refers you, they're putting a little bit of their own reputation on the line. Honor that trust. Celebrate it. And do it in a way that feels like you. Because the more joy and heart you bring to your recognition, the more people will want to be part of it.

And when you give the same high-quality care you gave to your referrer, then THEY become the hero because they are the ones who helped make it happen.

✦Own Your Magic ... AND Show It Off!✦

While we may not be able to directly ASK for referrals, we can absolutely thank our referrers ... publicly. This will not only encourage our referrers to *"keep 'em coming,"* it will also create buzz among their friends and family, who might just decide on their own to use you!

You will no longer need to *"chase"* business — **just let your brilliance be VISIBLE.**

> ## ANOTHER PUBLIC GRATITUDE IDEA
> Send a goodie (that can be shared) to your referrer's place of employment. Be sure to attach a note thanking them for the referral. It's a win-win for YOU, for your referrer, and for their friends!

🔑 Key Reflections

Who's one person I've never publicly thanked who made a real impact on my business?

_____
_____
_____

What fun or creative way can I celebrate a referrer this month?

_____
_____
_____
_____
_____

What could a *"Referral Rockstar"* program look like with my brand personality?

_____
_____
_____
_____
_____
_____
_____

NOTES

DOODLES

CHAPTER 7
Partnering for POWER

We are STRONGER and more SUCCESSFUL when we grow together.

One of the most powerful and underused tools in a thriving referral system is **partnership**. Think of your business not as a solo act, but as part of a high-vibe band, where every member brings their talents to the stage and amplifies everyone else's success.

In this chapter, we'll explore how to create aligned relationships with vendors, collaborators, and other professionals who want to refer you, and who would be thrilled to receive your referrals in return.

Let's build a referral ecosystem **that lifts everyone up.**

Vendor Referral Relationships

You already know how important your **preferred vendors** are. However, are you tapping into their referral potential?

Every time you send a client to your favorite lender, inspector, or moving company, you're building trust and loyalty. With a little intention, you can turn that relationship into a **referral partnership**.

Here's how:

- Be generous first. Send them business without strings attached.
- Follow up with a quick note: *"I love referring great clients to you. And I appreciate when you keep me in mind too."*
- Ask them who their ideal client is … and listen closely.
- Create a simple vendor list that includes your photo and referral language they can use when talking about you.

Example Text for Your Lender:

"Hey! I just added you to my vendor list that I give out to every new buyer. If you ever have someone who's not working with an agent yet, I'd be honored to help!"

It's all about **mutual respect** and communication, not pressure or expectation.

Co-Branded Events or Giveaways

If you want to go next-level with your partnerships, try teaming up for events or fun giveaways! These not only strengthen relationships but also bring in fresh eyes and new energy to both of your businesses.

Ideas:

- Host a spring-cleaning giveaway with your favorite organizer or handyperson.
- Partner with your lender for a *"Homebuyer Happy Hour"* or webinar.
- Co-sponsor a back-to-school supply drive or pet adoption event.
- Create a *"Welcome Home Basket"* program together for new buyers.

PRO TIP Co-brand your materials and share the spotlight equally. When vendors feel valued, they become excited champions of your brand.

How to Give Referrals Back

One of the best ways to receive referrals is to **give them freely and enthusiastically.**

People refer those who refer them.

Simple ways to do this:

- Keep a *"preferred partners"* list in your phone and share it often.
- Tag vendors on social media when you mention them. Public gratitude = loyalty.
- Drop their cards in client welcome packets
- Say their name out loud when clients ask for help, e.g., *"I've got the perfect painter for you."*

You don't need to track everything or formalize it. Just be generous and vocal. People will notice, and they'll remember you when the time comes.

PRO TIP Work with your vendor partners to create gift certificates for your clients that you can add to their closing gifts. Vendors will give YOU discounts for their services *(which you will buy)* and YOU will pass along FREE services to your clients in the form of gift certificates.

Forming a "Referral Circle" or Business Boosters Group

What if you had a go-to crew of like-minded professionals, each committed to supporting one another's success? That's exactly what a **Referral Circle** or **Business Boosters Group** can be.

Think of it as a small but mighty squad of trusted pros from different industries, all focused on building each other up — basically a **Referral Mastermind Group**.

How to create one:

- Invite 4–6 professionals you admire *(local or virtual)* from different fields: mortgage, insurance, home services, staging, coaching, marketing, etc.
- Meet once a month *(in person or via Zoom)*.
- Each meeting, spend 5 minutes per person sharing:
    - A quick win
    - A current challenge
    - A shoutout to another group member
    - An ideal referral you're looking for

You can also rotate hosts, co-host client appreciation events, or even swap social media spotlights.

The energy is electric when good people support one another. You don't need hundreds of people in your referral network, just the right ones.

Real Talk

You don't have to do this alone. You were never meant to. Your business can grow faster, more sustainably, and with more joy when you **invite others into the journey.**

Whether it's your favorite contractor or your go-to title rep, there are people who want to partner with you, and refer you, because you show up with heart and integrity.

Open the door. Build the bridge. Share the spotlight.

That's the power of partnership.

🔑 Key Reflections

Who are 3 professionals I could build stronger referral partnerships with?

_____
_____
_____

What's one way I could celebrate or support a vendor this week?

_____
_____
_____
_____

What kind of vendor referral collaboration would energize me? And who would I love to invite in?

_____
_____
_____
_____
_____
_____

NOTES

DOODLES

CHAPTER **8**

Events that SPARK Referrals

When was the last time you received something fun, unexpected, or meaningful, just because? That little spark of delight and intentionality is exactly what makes referral-based real estate marketing so powerful.

Events, pop-bys, and surprise-and-delight gestures don't have to be big or expensive to make a huge impression. In fact, when done with heart, even the simplest touchpoint can open the door for a warm referral.

This chapter is your go-to guide for creative, doable, and joy-filled events that generate buzz, deepen loyalty, and naturally encourage your clients, friends, and sphere to talk about you (and recommend you) with ease and excitement.

Pop-By Parties and Porch Surprises

Pop-bys are small, thoughtful deliveries to someone's door ... typically past clients, top referrers, or local friends in your sphere. They're personal, easy to prep, and fun to deliver. Want to level them up? Turn them into a mini-event or themed week!

Especially for Your Referrers:

- *"Gratitude on the Go"* – Deliver mini pumpkin pies before Thanksgiving with a tag like, *"I'm so THANKFUL for you — and your referrals!"*
- *"Spring Spark"* **Porch Surprise** – Drop off a potted flower with a note: *"Thanks for helping my business GROW. Who do you know that is ready to BLOOM into a new home?"*
- **Pop-by Picnic Bag** – Include lemonade mix, a couple of snacks, and a card with a sweet message like, *"You've got the referral magic! If there's anyone else in your world who could use a home matchmaker (ahem... me!), I'd love to help. Let's keep the good energy flowing."*

Want to deliver many in a day? Host a **Drive-Up Pick-Up** at a park or office, where people swing by to grab their goodies and say hi!

# Client Appreciation Parties with a Purpose

Your clients are your business's heartbeat, and celebrating them can be both joyful and strategic. Client appreciation events don't just say *"thank you."* When done intentionally, they create a ripple effect of **connection and referrals,** especially when you encourage everyone to bring with them someone who is thinking about buying or selling a home soon.

Event Ideas:

- **Ice Cream Social** – Rent a food truck or partner with a local creamery. Add a photo booth or raffle for a little flair!
- **Movie in the Park** – Invite clients and their families, provide popcorn, and offer branded picnic blankets or glow sticks.
- **Referrer VIP Night** – Host a more intimate gathering for your *"Top 25,"* with extra perks like wine tastings, charcuterie boards, or a gratitude toast.
- **"Bring a Friend" Bonus** – Encourage clients to invite a +1 who might be in the market or interested in real estate conversations.

Always include a short, heartfelt moment where you share how referrals sustain your business, and how much it means to you when people connect you with those they trust.

Birthday/Holiday Drop-Offs with Referral Reminders

Never underestimate the magic of just showing up, especially when it's aligned with a birthday or holiday!

Some Easy and Fun Examples:

- **Birthday Bag Drop** – Small gift, card, and a *"Wishing you a year full of love, joy, and endless FUN!"*
- **Valentine's Candy Gram** – *"Referrals are the sweetest gift you can give."*
- **Holiday Treat Box** – Homemade or locally sourced goodies with a message, *"Grateful for you this season — and always."*

These small acts create lasting impressions and gently keep you top of mind, without feeling salesy.

Creative Events with Low Cost, High Impact

You don't need a massive budget or huge guest list to host an event that shines.

Here are some **creative, high-impact ideas** that can easily spark referrals:

- **Shred-It Day** – Rent a shredding truck after tax season and invite clients to safely destroy old documents. Offer coffee and snacks while they wait.
- **Pumpkin Patch Meet-Up** – Offer a free pumpkin per family and a warm drink. Great photo ops = social shares = more visibility!

- **Back-to-School Survival Kit** – Drop off school supplies or treat bags to parents on your client list.
- **"Coffee's on Me" Day** – Partner with a local café and pay for the first 25 orders that mention your name. Then send texts to your Top 25 and tell them, *"Coffee's on Me!"* and where they can go to receive another thank you opportunity from you.

Each of these can include a referral nudge; a postcard, sign, text, or conversation like, *"I'd love to help someone you care about. Send them my way!"*

Keep It Personal, Not Promotional

What is the secret to events that spark referrals?

Those events don't feel like marketing.

They feel like **love, generosity, and connection.**

When your intention is to celebrate, uplift, and add value *(not to push or promote)*, people feel it. They remember it. And most importantly, they talk about it.

You become …
 more than a real estate agent.

You become …
 someone they're proud to recommend.

🔑 Key Reflections

What kind of event would be easy and fun for me to host?

_____
_____
_____
_____

Who are three people I'd love to surprise "just because" this month?

_____
_____
_____

What small, joyful gestures would make me feel valued if I were a client, customer, or referrer?

_____
_____
_____
_____
_____
_____
_____

NOTES

DOODLES

CHAPTER **9**

Market with a
REFERRAL MINDSET

Imagine This:

Every time someone sees your marketing, hears your name, or interacts with your content, they think not just, *"great real estate agent,"* but *"someone I'd feel confident referring to my friends."*

Gratitude is where the magic begins.

That's the power of marketing with a **referral mindset**.

When your brand, voice, and materials consistently reinforce your values and invite connection, referrals become a natural result, not a forced request.

 Let's explore how to infuse your marketing with referral **magic**.

Build Referral Language into Everything You Do

Instead of only asking for referrals occasionally, imagine your entire brand sending out attraction vibes.

"I grow through relationships."
"I treat referrals like gold."

Weave this mindset throughout your marketing.

Simple Phrases to Use:

- *"I'm never too busy for your referrals."*
- "When you share my name, you're opening doors — for me and for someone you care about."
- *"I love helping friends of friends—thank you for spreading the word!"*
- "Introductions from people I care about (like you!) are the heart of my business."

The above statements feel natural, not salesy. Use them in your connections and marketing materials:

- **Your Email signature**
- **Your brochures and postcards**
- **Buyer/seller guides**
- **Client gift tags**
- **Business cards**

They serve as a gentle reminder that you are open to and honored by referrals.

Your Website, Social, Voicemail, and More

Think of each of these as a digital handshake. They are an opportunity to say, *"I'd love to help the people you care about."*

Website

- Add a *"Refer a Friend"* tab or link in the main menu.
- Include stories or testimonials from clients who were referred.

Social Media Bios + Posts

- Biography example: *"Helping good people buy & sell homes with heart. Referrals always appreciated!"*
- Feature client success stories and talk about how they were introduced to you.
- Highlight referral partners *(vendors, mortgage pros, etc.)* with tags and gratitude.

Email Signature

Add a referral line below your name:

"Referrals are the heart of my business. Thank you for your trust!"

Voicemail Message

"Hi, this is [Your Name]. I'm helping amazing clients today, so leave your name, number, and how I can help. If you were referred to me, Welcome! I'll be contacting you soon!"

Social Media Posts That Inspire Sharing & Tagging

Referrals happen most often when people are reminded of you at the right time.

Use your posts to:

- Share client wins and thank referrers *(with permission)*.
- Celebrate "Referral Rockstars" monthly.
- Ask questions like:
    - *"Who's thinking of moving this year?"*
    - *"Tag a friend who needs help navigating the market!"*

Encourage playful participation:

- *"Tag someone who's dreaming of a bigger backyard!"*
- *"Know someone looking to buy but afraid of interest rates? Let's chat."*

And always include a soft **Call to Action**:

"DM me or send them my way. I'm happy to help!"

📰 Monthly Newsletter: Invite, Don't Sell

Newsletters are an ideal space to nurture relationships and organically encourage referrals.

Include:

- A warm letter or story from your life or recent work
- Tips & trends for buyers/sellers
- Shoutouts for recent referrals
- A section like: **Client Love Corner** – *"Thank you to Sarah L. for introducing me to your sister! Referrals like yours mean everything."*
- An invite to your **Referral Rewards Program** or next **pop-by party** or **client appreciation event**.

Don't forget to include something fun, personal, or delightful:

- Favorite local coffee shop
- Behind-the-scenes photos
- Book or podcast recommendation
- Fun *"Forward this to a friend who needs…"* blurbs

The tone of your newsletter should always be relational and helpful over transactional.

Marketing with a referral mindset isn't about shouting *"Send me clients!"* It's about staying present, showing heart, and becoming so trusted that people naturally connect others to you.

🔑 Key Reflections

How can I infuse genuine gratitude and referral-friendly language into my everyday marketing?

_____
_____
_____
_____

What small updates could I make to my website, voicemail, or newsletter that invite people to think of me when a referral opportunity arises?

_____
_____
_____
_____
_____

What does *"sharing from the heart"* look like on social media for me?

_____
_____
_____
_____
_____

NOTES

DOODLES

CHAPTER 10

Keep Up the Momentum

You've set your **referral foundation.** You've built a rhythm. You've celebrated, shared, and shined.

CONSISTENCY compounds. What you nurture grows.

But the key to a thriving, joyful, and sustainable referral-based business is this:

Keep the magic flowing...

This chapter is about **momentum**. It's about keeping your systems humming and your heart connected. It's about fueling your business in a way that feels abundant, not exhausting.

Set Monthly or Quarterly Referral Goals

Think of goals as guideposts, not pressure points.

Setting a clear *(and fun!)* intention, like 3 referrals per month or 10 strong referrals per quarter, gives you something to stretch toward. But rather than tying your self-worth to the outcome, let your goal be an invitation to show up, stay visible, and stay connected.

PRO TIP Track your goals somewhere visible; on a whiteboard, in your planner, or even with a colorful jar of marbles. Make it tactile. Make it yours.

Review, Refine, and Refresh Your Rewards Program

Your referral rewards shouldn't go stale, or feel like a chore. Schedule a quarterly check-in with yourself to look over what's working and what's not. Ask:

- Are my referrers still excited by the rewards I'm offering?
- What reward did people mention or remember most?
- What felt joyful to give?
- What reward ideas do I want to try next?

Seasons change, and so can your program. Add a surprise twist. Introduce a new tier. Switch out the chocolate for candles, or the coffee card for a flower delivery. Keep it fresh and fun.

Re-Engage with Your Under-the-Radar Referrers

Some people loved working with you... and then went quiet.

That doesn't mean they don't care. Life gets busy. People move, have babies, change jobs. Your role is to gently re-spark the connection.

Here are a few light, non-salesy ways to check in:

- "Hi Jenny! I was thinking of you today and just wanted to say hello. I hope your backyard garden is blooming beautifully again this year. Please send photos!"

- "I'm sharing a fun monthly newsletter now. I'd love to add you to the list. Would that be okay?"

- "Hey Daniel! It's been a bit. If you're still loving your home, I'd enjoy seeing a pic of what you've done with it. I know you had some big plans for that new theater room."

No pressure.

Just presence.

🤾 Avoiding Burnout: Keep it Joyful, Not Overwhelming

Let's be honest: even care-driven business owners can get tired. The key is designing systems that support you, not deplete you.

Protect your joy by:

- Batching your outreach tasks on one fun afternoon per month *(music on, snacks ready!)*.
- Using automation where it helps *(email scheduling, birthday reminders)*.
- Delegating where needed *(hire help to send thank-you gifts or prep pop-bys)*.
- Letting go of perfection. It doesn't have to be flawless to be felt.

Remember, referrals flow best when you feel good. Your energy is your brand.

You're not just creating a business. You're nurturing a beautiful, referral-powered rhythm.

And like anything living and breathing—it just needs your love, light, and a little ongoing care.

🗝️ Key Reflections

What is a realistic and joyful referral goal I want to set for this season?

_____
_____
_____
_____

What reward or gesture have I given that made me smile the most?

_____
_____
_____
_____
_____

Who is one past client I'd love to reconnect with this month—and how can I make it heartfelt?

_____
_____
_____
_____
_____

NOTES

NOTES

DOODLES

CONCLUSION

Building a Business with HEART

Let's pause for a moment and breathe it in.

You've just walked through an entire framework for growing a referral-based business, one rooted in **gratitude, connection, and heart**.

You now know how to:

- Invite referrals with ease and intention
- Celebrate your referrers in meaningful ways
- Follow up in ways that feel aligned *(not automated)*
- Stay visible and valuable in your clients' lives
- And create momentum that keeps flowing joyfully

Now it's time to trust it. And trust yourself.

Gratitude Is the Secret Sauce

If there's one golden thread that runs through every chapter, it's **Gratitude**. Not just the polite *"thank-you"* kind, but the deeper kind. The kind that says:

> *"I see you... I appreciate you... You matter to my business and to me."*

When people feel that kind of acknowledgment, they remember it. They're moved by it.

And more often than not... they respond to it.

Your Business Grows at the Speed of Your Generosity

You don't have to hustle harder or outshine everyone else in your market. You just need to be generous ... with your attention, appreciation, and energy.

A generous business is magnetic. It pulls people in. And it creates a ripple effect of goodwill that grows far beyond your marketing plan.

See Your Future Referral Pipeline Flowing Effortlessly

Imagine this:

- Your inbox holds new referrals from happy clients who *"just had to tell someone about you."*
- Your community begins to see you not only as a real estate professional, but as someone they trust and admire.

- Your business feels joyful, spacious, and energizing.
- You wake up excited to serve, not burned out from doing "all the things."

This isn't a fantasy… It's what happens when you **build your business with heart.**

♡ A Final Pep Talk *(from me to you)*

You don't need to be louder, pushier, or more polished. You just need to be you … kind, real, consistent, and willing.

Willing to **show up**. Willing to **give**. Willing to keep **choosing connection** over perfection.

Your clients already love you.

Now it's time to let the world know what kind of magic happens when people send their friends and family your way.

You're not just building a referral system. You're building a legacy of caring.

Let's keep the magic flowing.

With heart,

Donna ♡

NOTES

 MORE MAGIC

For those who luuuuuuv the extras, here are some Bonus Materials to assist you as you create or refresh your real estate marketing plan. Enjoy!

BONUS: Reward Ideas for Every Budget

Whether you're just getting started or celebrating a booming referral business, there's always a thoughtful way to say thank you. Here's a mix of meaningful and magical rewards to inspire your giving:

Budget-Friendly ($0–$10)

- **Custom Bookmark** – Design one with an inspiring quote or their name.
- **Mini Succulent** – A small plant with a big message: *"Thanks for helping me grow!"*
- **Printed Photo Memory** – Frame a photo from your last event or closing.
- **Digital Gift** *(E-book or Playlist)* – Curate your favorite reads or tunes.
- **Homemade Treat** – Think cookies in a jar or a signature snack.
- **Desk Affirmation Card** – Something uplifting to keep nearby.
- **"You Are Appreciated" Tag** – Attach to any simple goodie *(candle, soap, chocolate)*.

Mid-Range ($10–$40)

- **Locally Made Goodies** – Honey, jam, or artisan soaps with a personal note.
- **Branded Swag** – Cute mugs, tote bags, or water bottles with your logo and vibe.
- **Self-Care Box** – Curate with journal, oils, cozy socks.
- **Movie Night Kit** – Popcorn, candy, and a movie streaming gift card.
- **Candle with Meaning** – Choose a scent with a symbolic name like "Gratitude" or "Joy."
- **Lunch on You** – Send a DoorDash or UberEats gift card with a note that says, *"Lunch is my treat!"*

Premium ($50+)

- **Dinner for Two** – A generous restaurant or meal delivery gift card.
- **Spa or Massage Voucher** – Encourage rest and renewal.
- **Home Decor Gift** – pretty tea towels, a framed quote, or cozy throw.
- **Subscription Box** – for wine, books, candles, or snacks.
- **Tickets to an Experience** – Movie night, escape room, art class—something local and fun.
- **Personalized Gift** – Monogrammed tote, cutting board, or wine glass with their name or closing date.

PRO TIP The most magical rewards are the ones that reflect you and your relationship with your referrer. Add a little sparkle, a personal note, or even a playful theme—and you'll be unforgettable.

BONUS: 12 Months of Referral Marketing Ideas

A year of simple, soulful connection with your favorite people:

January – New Year, New Home Vibes

Theme: Fresh Starts

Idea: Send out a *"New Year, New Dreams"* postcard or email and include a prompt: *"Know someone with big home goals this year? I'd love to help make them real."* Include a mini home goals checklist or a digital vision board template.

February – Love & Loyalty

Theme: Love Notes + Loyalty

Idea: Handwrite 5–10 appreciation cards for past referrers or top clients. Include a *"You're on my VIP List"* message and a coffee or treat gift card.

March – Spring into Action

Theme: Fresh Energy

Idea: Host a **Spring Referral Refresh** pop-by with seed packets or flower bulbs. Tagline: *"Help me grow my business—plant a referral!"*

April – Client Appreciation Drive-Up

Theme: Celebration

Idea: Organize a **Grab & Go Goodies** event. Clients / referrers swing by for snacks or goodies. Offer referral cards they can take to pass along.

May – Mother's Day Magic

Theme: Care and Connection

Idea: Drop off *(or mail)* mini succulents or flower tea bags with a tag: *"Referrals make my business bloom. Thank you for helping it grow!"*

June – Summer Kickoff

Theme: Fun in the Sun

Idea: **"Unannounced" Referral Contest** *(since we don't solicit referrals)*. Prize ideas: picnic set, s'mores kit, pool float, local restaurant gift card. Post: *"Guess who sent me the most referrals for the first half of the year? Thank you! And here's a fun gift to show you my appreciation for your trust in me!"*

July – Freedom to Refer

Theme: Fireworks + Freedom

Idea: Run a social media game where people tag someone they know who's moving soon. Also a great time for festive porch pop-bys with sparklers or mini flags.

August – Back to Cool

Theme: Reconnect + Reset

Idea: Check in with *"quiet"* clients with a kind message: *"Thinking of you this season. If you or someone you care about has plans that include a move soon, I'd love to help."*

September – Gratitude in Action

Theme: Service + Support

Idea: Highlight your favorite vendors! Tag local handy-people, stagers, or cleaners and ask them to do the same. It builds your network and cross-referral energy.

October – Treat Your Referrers

Theme: Sweet Surprises

Idea: Porch drop a Halloween treat with a note: *"No tricks, just a heartfelt thank you for your support this year!"*

November – Gratitude Month

Theme: Thankfulness

Idea: Launch a **Gratitude Giveaway** just for your referrers. Post a list of names *(or initials)* and say: *"You've helped my business this year and I am sooo thankful. Watch for a gratitude this month!"*

December – Cheers to You!

Theme: Celebration

Idea: Send a personalized holiday card or small gift to your top referrers. Add a note: *"My year was brighter because of you. Thank you for sending good people my way."*

BONUS: Sample Pop-By Ideas

Creative connection gifts help spark smiles and referrals. These pop-by ideas are low-cost, high-impact, and easy to personalize. Add a cute tag, a handwritten note, and maybe your business card or magnet. Then let your magic do the rest!

Spring Pop-Bys

- *"Bloom Where You're Planted"* — Mini potted flowers or seed packets
- *"Just Popping By to Plant Some Gratitude"* — Flower bulbs with a colorful ribbon
- *"I'm Egg-cited to Help with All Your Real Estate Needs!"* — Fill a plastic egg or mini basket with candy

Summer Pop-Bys

- *"You're the Bomb!"* – Bag of mini firecracker pops or a bath bomb
- *"You Make My Business Sizzle!"* – Grill seasoning, BBQ sauce, or a hot sauce mini pack
- *"Your Referrals Keep Me Afloat"* – Pool float keychain, pool float toy, or sunscreen

Fall Pop-Bys

- *"Fall-ing for Great Clients Like You"* – Mini pumpkin or spiced candle
- *"I'm Thankful for You!"* – Caramel apples, mini pie, or gourmet popcorn
- *"Donut Know What I'd Do Without You"* – Box of donut holes or a single gourmet donut

Winter Pop-Bys

- *"You Warm My Heart"* – Hot cocoa packet, mug, or tea sampler
- *"It's SNOW Nice to Work with You"* – Snowflake ornament or fuzzy socks
- *"Wishing You a SWEET Season"* – Holiday cookies, candy canes, or a candy bar with a bow

Real Estate-Themed Anytime Pop-Bys

- *"Thanks for Helping My Business GROW"* – Succulent in a small pot
- *"You're the KEY to My Success"* – Key-shaped bottle opener or keychain
- *"I'm Grateful for YOU Keeping ME in Mind"* – Notepad, sticky notes, or mini journal
- *"Thanks for Helping Me BUILD My Business"* – Small LEGO house or building block set *(fun for families!)*

Just Because …

- *"Here's a Little Happy!"* – Mini candy jar or treat bag
- *"Hope This Brightens Your Day"* – Colorful highlighters, lip balm, or candles
- *"You're Simply the BEST!"* – Gift card for coffee, local bakery, or frozen yogurt

BONUS: Referral Roadmap

Here are the steps to turn authentic connection into consistent referrals:

Attract
Be visible. Be valuable. Be you.

- Share stories and helpful content on social media
- Show up in community spaces and local events
- Use branded print touchpoints *(postcards, newsletters, client gifts)*
- Be top-of-mind with seasonal pop-bys and thoughtful gestures
- **Be the lighthouse**, not the megaphone

Connect
Create real conversation, not cold contact.

- Comment and celebrate others on social media
- Send handwritten notes or texts to check in
- Invite past clients to coffee or a small gathering
- Offer value with no strings attached *(guides, checklists, updates)*
- Ask how they're doing. **Listen first, pitch never**

Serve
Deliver excellence with soul.

- Create a memorable client experience from hello to closing
- Use systems to stay in flow *(buyer and seller campaigns, client care checklists, email follow-ups)*

- Infuse delight into each step *(surprise gifts, celebration moments)*
- Educate and empower your clients
- Stay tuned into **what matters most to them**

Invite
Gently ask. Sincerely appreciate.

- Ask for referrals with scripts that feel good
- Share stories of past clients who were referred
- Let people know how grateful you are for their trust
- Use warm language: *"I love helping your friends and family!"*
- **Make it easy:** provide cards, digital links, social reminders, text referral together for the intro

Reward
Celebrate and acknowledge.

- Send a thoughtful thank you for each referral
- Create a referral rewards program or VIP club
- Publicly recognize referrers when appropriate
- Deliver heartfelt appreciation, not generic gifts
- Reinforce how their referral helps your business thrive

Repeat
Keep the momentum flowing.

- Schedule regular check-ins with your sphere
- Keep giving value between transactions
- Stay consistent in marketing touchpoints
- Reflect on what's working and where you can uplevel
- Nourish the relationships. They are the roots of your business

BONUS: Self-Care for the Referral Rockstar

You give so much to others; your clients, your colleagues, your community. But your best referrals and biggest breakthroughs happen when you're aligned, energized, and well cared for.

Here's your gentle permission slip *(and power plan)* to take care of you ... mind, body, heart, and soul.

Daily Practices

- **Morning Mindset Boost:** Start your day with one minute of gratitude. *"I am open to receiving love, leads, and referrals today."*
- **Move Your Energy:** 10 minutes of movement; stretch, dance, walk, shake it off.
- **Hydration + Nourishment:** Fuel your body like the powerhouse it is. Don't skip lunch for showings.
- **Boundaries Are Beautiful:** Set work hours. Honor quiet time. Say no with grace when it's a no for you.

Weekly Recharge Rituals

- **Referral-Free Zone:** Create a space *(or a time slot)* in your week that is completely yours. No clients. No marketing. Just you.
- **Soul Soak or Spa Moment:** Bath, facial, tea time, or a solo coffee shop date. Whatever feels indulgent and restorative.

Monthly Self-Care Check In

- Am I working in alignment with my values?
- Do I need more rest, inspiration, or connection right now?
- What's one loving thing I can do for myself this month?

Remember:

Burnout doesn't build referrals, alignment does. You are not just a real estate agent. You are a life changer, a community builder, a connector with heart.

So, take exquisite care of your most valuable asset:

YOU!

ABOUT THE AUTHOR

Donna Wysinger began her real estate career over 25 years ago with a simple curiosity about flipping homes. What started as a personal interest quickly grew into helping friends and family buy and sell properties.

Though she hadn't planned on becoming a full-time Realtor, Donna soon realized that true success would only come by trusting herself and going all in. She immersed herself in the industry, learning every aspect of the business while working alongside top agents and on highly successful teams. Over the years she has worn many hats: listing specialist, buyer guide, transaction coordinator, admin support, new homes specialist, marketing designer and coordinator, new agents trainer, new assistants trainer, and more.

With her strong background in design and marketing, Donna also helped countless agents grow their businesses by creating resources and tools that helped them stand out. Eventually, she partnered with her sister to build a thriving real estate business of her own, using the very systems and strategies she had been developing and teaching. Together, they built not only sales, but lasting relationships within their community.

Today, after more than a quarter century in the industry, Donna has distilled her knowledge and experience into the **Be a Better Agent** community and her series of quick-read guidebooks. Her mission is simple: to help real estate professionals grow with confidence, connection, and ease.

MORE BOOKS in the Mini Mastery Series

If you enjoyed this guide, you'll love all of Donna's handbooks for real estate professionals. Each book is concise, practical, and designed to give you great resources you can use right away. Scan this QR code to explore all of her books on Amazon. *And she's still creating more!*

www.ingramcontent.com/pod-product-compliance
Lightning Source LLC
Chambersburg PA
CBHW071146090426
42736CB00012B/2248